Rescuing Vintage Textiles

Rescuing Vintage Textiles

Mary Beth Temple

St. Johann Press
Haworth, NJ

Library of Congress Cataloging-in-Publication Data

Temple, Mary Beth.
    Rescuing vintage textiles / Mary Beth Temple.
    p. cm.
    Includes bibliographical references and index.
    ISBN 1-878282-09-3 (acid-free paper)
      1. Textile fabrics—Conservation and restoration. 2. Textile fabrics—
    Cleaning. I. Title.

    NK8804.5.T463 2000
    746'.028'8—dc21   00-026047

Author photo styled by Jill Merritt
Author photo by Neal Clipper, Abbey Photographers

Contents

Dedication

Thanks to John S. Temple, my favorite copy editor, and to Katie Temple for helping with Mommy's "pretties." Also, my thanks to the McCabe family and all its extensions, Debbie Bonito and Key Mertens for unstinting sharing of their love for and knowledge of linens, and to David and Diane Biesel of St. Johann Press.

Introduction

It seems I have been interested in fabrics all of my life. I remember my mother teaching me to sew, my sister Trish teaching me to knit, and my sister Judith interesting me in fancy needlework. When the other eighth graders were bitterly complaining about the relevance of school projects about life in Colonial America, I was happily trying to make what I thought an eighteenth-century sampler should look like. I had never seen one except in books, but the thought intrigued me. No matter what avenues of employment I have tried, I always wend my way back to textiles and sewing. In short, it is a subject I am passionate about.

I started collecting and selling vintage textiles in a roundabout way. After buying a turn-of-the-century house and spending all of my available cash at closing, I started haunting local estate sales, searching for bargain period furnishings. At the time, I was working in costumes (as I have since 1984) on a Broadway musical. I went to an estate sale at a Victorian house in Hasbrouck Heights, New Jersey, and discovered a wicker laundry basket filled with beautifully made table linens. I was appalled (on the items' behalf) at how they were being treated—sets separated, napkins dropped on the floor and left there, no respect given them at all! I made a deal with the proprietor, at a price I couldn't really afford, and took them all home with me—my first "rescue." I put aside what I couldn't live without and started thinking about how to get rid of the items that I couldn't keep in a way befitting their dignity.

I decided to sell them at a local auction, but a friend at work mentioned that she was looking for a few nice doilies and dresser scarves. She had heard me talk about my daring textile rescue and asked if she could look at a few and pay me for what she wanted. An actor overheard our conversation and said he was looking for a few small pieces as well. I washed two dozen pieces and put them in individual zippered bags, a thought that makes me cringe now, and put them in a vintage suitcase I had purchased the week before. During the dinner break between shows on a matinee day I sold enough to pay for half of the lot—and I still had many pieces left. A business was born! I took linens to other Broadway shows, used the proceeds to buy more linens, then graduated to setting up at small antique shows. The rest, as they say, is history. I still have that vintage linen suitcase, but these days it holds about 1 percent of my stock.

Along the way I tried every stain removal technique I ever heard about and slowly developed a system that works and some ideas about what doesn't. Soon I realized that I spent a large portion of the time I was set up at antique shows talking about how to take care of the things people bought from me, and usually even more time trying to explain how best to take care of the textiles they had found in their mothers' attic. A promoter noticed this trend and asked me to lecture at some of her shows. As I started to write down lecture notes, and as the lectures got longer and more detailed, this book was born.

I hope that when you read this book you will get some ideas on how to examine and care for the linens and textiles you inherit from family members or pieces you find at garage sales, where the uninitiated treat them poorly! I'm sure you've seen the popular TV shows where appraisers cheerfully announce that the silver bucket found in the attic is a priceless antique, but not everyone with an interest in times past is going to be left a fortune. What many of us are left with is our mother's or grandmother's or great-aunt's embroidered pillowcases, the christening gown our fathers wore, the tablecloth from whatever "old country" our parents or grandparents happen to be from. And I am here to tell you that those *are* priceless treasures, even if they don't sell for millions on the Internet auctions. These items were treasured and loved by our forebears and give a brief glimpse into the lives they led. They deserve to be taken care of and treasured, "rescued" if you will, and passed on to those who follow in our footsteps.

If you need further information on supplies or wish to have a specific question answered, please visit my Website: www.marybethtemple.com

Chapter 1
The Big Five: Cotton, Linen, Wool, Silk, and Rayon

Most vintage or antique textiles are made from one of the "Big Five"—cotton, linen, wool, silk, or rayon. In this chapter I will give you some identifying characteristics of these fibers and mention the types of items you are likely to find in each material. This information is meant to give you an idea of what you are looking at when sorting through your textiles. But for more information check your local library for a textile history book. You will become addicted!

Linen, possibly the oldest of the spun fibers, is often found in table and bed linens. It is the only fiber that is stronger wet than dry, so it responds relatively well to being washed. Known for its properties of wicking and absorbency, this is what bath and hand towels were made of before cotton terry cloth became popular. Even into the 1940s and 50s, linen kitchen towels were prized because they do not leave lint when drying glass or china. You will often find vintage towels with the words "Glass towel" woven into the pattern. Made

Residue of burnt cotton fabric

Residue of burnt rayon fabric

in the linen-producing centers of Ireland, Czechoslovakia, and Austria, among others, the older damask tablecloths are treasured for the luster and gloss of the finish and the intricacy of the subject and patterns. Although these cloths are most often found in white and off-white, some terrific colors can still be discovered, especially from Czechoslovakia, and several patterns can be found that are white-centered with a colored border. Linen sheets and pillowcases are terrific finds. Try sleeping on "real" bed linens in the summer and you will never go back!

As well as the glossy, manufactured fancy dress cousins, items made of homespun linen are often found in your grandmother's cedar chest, especially if your ancestors lived in a rural area. Look for a coarse, slightly irregular weave, center seams in sheets or tablecloths—the home looms were not always as wide as the desired finished piece, so two or more widths had to be seamed together—or stripes that are not all the same number of threads wide. Stripes were often done "by eye" or by the look of things rather than by being precisely measured out. Homespuns are predominately natural in color, sometimes with a check or a stripe.

It's very difficult for me to teach you in a book how to recognize linen from cotton. Often I can tell from the feel or look of a weave, but you can't very well feel a photo in this book. Take a field trip to your local fabric store and browse. Today's fabrics are required to be labeled for fiber content, the same way your clothes are. Look at some of the fabrics that catch your eye, feel them, then read the fiber content on the end of the bolt. Antique linen dealers can be a great resource, too. I am always comparing linen sheets with cotton ones for people who are trying to learn the difference.

One way people identify fiber content is by using the burn test. Simply put, several threads from a textile are burned in a flame (not a match), the smell and resulting residue are analyzed, and a determination is made. I have used this method for relatively new fabrics while trying to weed out all-cotton prints from cotton-polyester blends when they are found in an unlabeled stack. Even a novice can see the difference in the residue: Items with any type of synthetic fiber in them leave a melted-looking residue that hardens; natural fibers leave what looks like ash. However, I think you would have to use this test many times on different pieces (some of which you know in advance what the fiber is) to learn how to determine fiber content accurately. Differences in the odors or ashes might be slight, and only with a great deal of personal experience is this test fast and accurate.

Cotton is another fiber found everywhere. Tablecloths and napkins, bed linens, lacy curtains, paisley prints from India, checked bedspreads, yards of dress fabric–all are, or can be, made of cotton. Sometimes it is very difficult to date a piece of fabric. The pattern of a newer one may have been copied from a much older piece. For example, familiarizing yourself with different styles of decorating (Arts and Crafts, Art Deco, Art Nouveau, etc.) will give you a feel for approximate ages of some items. Textile design was often related to styles in furniture and home decor. A little knowledge of Roman numerals can help you out here as well. I have occasionally been drawn to a piece of beautifully designed fabric in excellent condition, only to find on closer inspection of the selvage that it was milled in 1985 (MCMLXXXV)!

Width of the fabric can also give you a clue. While not a hard-and-fast rule, the earlier a fabric was milled, the narrower it is. When I was learning to sew in the 1960s, most patterns for the home sewer offered layout diagrams in both 36-inch and 45-inch-wide fabric, because those were the widths that were readily available. Today most fabrics are 45 inches wide or wider, and a 36-inch-wide piece is a rarity or a specialty good.

Woolen goods are not likely to take up much of your collection at this time. I have had some interesting wool fabrics turn up in utility quilts and colored woven coverlets from the nineteenth century. Generally, however, if you are sorting through your mother's or grandmother's household goods, wool will not take up a large percentage of the items, excluding clothing. Older homespun woolen items can have an almost greasy feel to them, because wool was often spun directly as it came from the sheep and was washed after it was turned into yarn. Spinning with the lanolin still in the wool is easier, and leaving some lanolin in the wool can make the resulting garment a bit water resistant. Wool is particularly susceptible to insect damage, as you know if you ever were less than careful in putting away your winter sweaters for the summer! Thus, few wool items have remained safely stored over a long period of time.

Silk is the luxury fabric. Spun from the filaments of many tiny silkworm cocoons, it has a unique gloss and drape. While silk production has been around for centuries, discovering antique and vintage silk in good condition is increasingly rare. More than the other natural fibers, silk is susceptible to dry rot and can shatter to dust if handled after improper storage. This is one of the reasons Victorian crazy quilts in good condition are so highly prized—crazy quilts often had bright silk patches in them, and silks are likely to shatter. The dyes used in producing colored silks in the eighteenth century have an even harsher effect on the silk than does dryness. Particularly in black, reds, and browns, the dyes were set using salt—not an aid to textile longevity. Heavier silks made for drapes and upholstery have a better chance of lasting than do dress-weight goods. Sometimes heavier silks have a warp thread of cotton or linen, and if the drapes were lined to keep them away from the damaging rays of the sun, they stand a chance of surviving. Even fabric from damaged silk drapes is desirable for making pillows or reupholstering period furniture.

Which leads us to rayon. Rayon was invented in 1884 as an artificial silk by the French inventor and industrialist Hilaire Chardonnet. He and others wanted to bring the gloss and colors, not to mention cachet, of silk to the masses, but without the high prices. The term *rayon* itself was coined in the United States in 1924. It is cellulose based, like plant fibers, yet it is a manufactured thread. Don't sneer at rayon just because it's newer. It's been around longer than most people think, and a lot of time was put into making the earlier pieces look "just like silk." Some items from the 1930s and 1940s have terrific design detail in them, particularly the bedspreads and figural fabrics milled in Italy before World War II. Post WWII Japan produced some very interesting cotton/rayon blend tablecloths and napkins. While not particularly valuable in terms of textile collecting, they are still to be found in a multitude of colors and sizes, and some of the weaves are quite striking.

While sorting through the textile items you think you want to work on, try to take an educated guess as to which item is made of which fiber.

Now let's move on to assessing an item's condition.

Chapter 2
Assessing a Specific Item

You have chosen an item from your collection and want to rescue it. Where do you begin?

The first thing you need to think about before you get into anything technical is: How do I want this piece to look when I am through fooling with it? Keep in mind that every process you put a textile through increases the chance that you will hurt it. You always want to do the least to an item that you possibly can to get your desired result. Remember that is going to vary from piece to piece. In some cases you will assess the item and decide that the best thing you can do for it is to store it properly and leave it alone.

Anything you do will follow from the answer to this one simple question: Do I want to conserve it or restore it? Webster's says conservation is "a careful preservation and protection of something. . . ." Webster's also says restoration is "a bringing back to a former position or condition. . . ." The shorthand I always use is this: Conservation is keeping it as it *is*; restoration is making it like it *was*.

- Do you want your grandmother's quilt to pass from generation to generation, warts and all, because it shows that it was well-loved and used? Conserve it.

- Do you want your grandmother's quilt to be shown off and slept under in the guest room in a condition as close to its original splendor as possible, even if it means adding some contemporary fabrics? Restore it.

- Is a piece of eighteenth-century lace going to be added to your collection for its historical value, or for you to study its make-up? Conserve it.

- Is that filet lace tablecloth going on display in your formal dining room, preferably without the ghosts of turkey dinners past? Restore it.

What you want to do with an item ultimately affects the decisions you will make about how to care for it. Why you are saving some things will also influence that decision. You will have a greater emotional attachment to the embroidered pillowcases that great-aunt Mabel brought from the old country than you will to the stained, but interesting, tablecloth that you picked up at a garage sale, By the same token, something that you want for your collection because it is interesting in its manufacture will not be treated the same way as something you actually want to use in your home. We are talking here to some degree about risk tolerance. I would always rather have a faint stain than any kind of hole, but I am always aware that washing anything leaves a possibility that the item won't hold up under water, no matter how gentle I am trying to be and what kind of soap I am using. Ask yourself: How do I want an item to end up? When you get there, *stop*. If you are happy with the result, you are finished.

Another question you will need to answer is: What fiber is this item made of? You have read chapter 1, so of course you can figure this out in your sleep, or you have snagged some threads and burned them to help you along. Fiber content has a lot to do with which cleaning products and methods you are going to use. Don't get lazy here. When you have ascertained that the pretty runner is a natural colored linen, don't forget to consider the make-up of the colored embroidery threads used for decoration. Are they silk or cotton or even wool? Are there sequins or beads or buttons applied to it? Whatever you are doing to a piece, you are doing to all of it. This concept will come up a lot in the chapter on quilts.

How was this item made? With hand embroidery or a printed design? With lots of cutwork and drawn threads or as one solid panel? Anything that cuts into the work violates the integrity of the base fabric, which is a fancy way of saying the more holes that are in it (even on purpose), the more likely it is to rip when being cleaned.

Approximately how old is it? Remember, poor storage can make a 1950s piece look terrible, and proper storage can keep a nineteenth-century heirloom looking younger longer. A general rule of thumb is the older the piece the more delicate it is and the fewer processes you want to put it through.

One of the best and fastest ways to analyze a piece of fabric for damage is to hold it up to a strong light and look through it. Strong sunlight works best, but halogen lights are good too. Holes, even tiny ones, will jump out at you because the light is coming through the fabric without hindrance. Areas that are "thin" will jump out at you too. These are spots that show some wear and, if not cared for properly, will develop holes. You can also see stains this way—even very light ones. Check every piece you want to work on very carefully and take note of what you see and where you see it. Now look at the piece from the front and note any places where the surface decoration looks loose or has some threads pulled out. Look again from the back and see if there are any loose threads there. Anything that looks like a potential problem area needs to be stabilized before cleaning.

Once you have figured out where all the stains are, it is a good idea to take a guess as to what caused them. Make-up of the stain, as well as fiber content, help you decide which cleaning product to use. Is the stain basically round with irregular edges and about halfway between the center and the edge of a tablecloth? More than likely that's a food stain. Yellowing in the center of a pillowcase—often one of a pair? Hair oil. Straight lines of yellowish discoloration along the folds? Poor storage, or what I refer to as "closet crud." Black or brown, organic-looking discoloration? Mold. Each of these is handled a bit differently. Sometimes you just can't tell, and that's okay, too, but any bit of information you can gather along the way helps this process along, enabling you to do as little as possible to solve each problem.

Does this piece have dry rot? Dry rot results from a lack of humidity caused by poor storage. Any fiber can have this problem, but silks in particular are prone to it. When you handle a dry-rotted item it disintegrates or crumbles into dust. Silks can split into vertical lines, or "shatter." Unfortunately dry rot is irreversible. If you are desperate to save a dry-rotted item, the best you can do is mount it (see the next chapter) and store it properly.

If, after assessing an item, you decide that you are out of your league, don't know where to begin, are terrified of doing something to harm it, have so much sentimental attachment

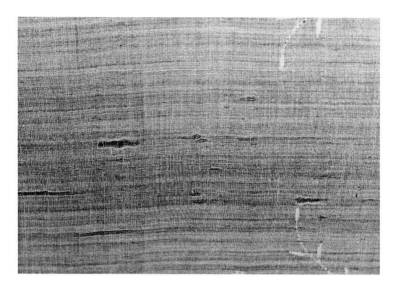

Thin spots that can lead to major damage

Dry rot is irreversible

to it that you do not want to handle it, think it's exceedingly financially valuable or several hundred years old—stop and call a professional conservator. This book, no matter how well intentioned, is going to make you a well-informed amateur, not a professional with years of experience. If you need help, get it. You can always try your skill later with another piece.

Remember, even with the best of care, fiber is an organic material and therefore was never meant to last forever. Our job, as people who love it and take care of it, is to keep it in the best condition we can and share our love of these items with the next generation.

Chapter 3
Stabilizing Damage Before Cleaning

Now that you have chosen a project, we need to start work. Before any cleaning begins, the item you are working on must be stabilized to prevent foreseeable damage. Some problems may occur that were not foreseeable, but this way you have done the best you can to prevent any new damage.

What do I mean by stabilize? You are going to add another piece of fabric, permanently or temporarily, to the damaged area to strengthen it. Washing an item with a hole in it is asking for trouble, because the area around the hole will rip or fray very quickly. Putting a piece with even a one-quarter-inch hole in the wash is likely to leave you with a piece that has a foot-long tear. I cannot stress this enough: Never put any item with an unstabilized hole in it through the stress of being laundered. Thin spots should be reinforced as well, because the fibers here are already weaker than normal, and this is the first area where a new hole will begin.

The first question you want to ask yourself is: Is this a permanent or a temporary repair? For example, with a thin spot that may cover a fairly large area, you want to baste a piece of fabric over the thin area to take some of the stress of laundering off of the item. When you are finished washing and drying this item, you probably don't need that patch anymore and it would look much nicer displayed with it off. That's a temporary patch.

However, if grandma's tablecloth has some damage in the cutwork of the center medallion, you will want to stabilize that area forever, not just for this one wash. That would call for a permanent patch.

What kind of fabric should you use? For a temporary patch, the best bet is unbleached muslin. It is sturdy, readily available, and inexpensive. After you buy it at the fabric store you should wash it to get all of the sizing and chemicals out of it. Wash it twice, then you can throw it in the dryer. Give it a quick iron to get out the major wrinkles, then you are ready to go.

For a permanent repair we go back to the question of conservation or restoration. Again we are asking whether you want to keep it as it is or make it like it was. One of the things that struck me when I traveled through Hungary in the late 1980s was the way the architectural items at the museum in Buda Castle had been mended. The conservation department had in fact added material to the partial pieces where they thought it might belong, but there was no attempt to hide the fact that the addition was an addition. Often the addition was a different color than the artifact, so you could see where the original left off and where the guesswork began. In this same way, you might want to put a permanent patch on a textile piece, but will want to make it clear what is original to the item and what is not. In that case, a patch of unbleached muslin, prepared as above, makes the most sense. If you want to bring the piece back to where it was, you may want to shop for a fabric as close as possible to what you think the original was.

The search for a fabric that you want to blend in can be as extensive as your options allow. Check out antique dealers and garage sales in your area for items from the same time period as the piece you are working on. Often you can pick up a "cutter"—a piece that is already so badly damaged you wouldn't mind cutting into it for a project—for a low price. Make sure that any vintage fabric you find is strong and shows no sign of dry rot. If you try to patch an unstable area with an unstable fabric, you will just waste your time in the long run. A little fading can be good, however, if it matches the overall condition of the piece you are working on. Wash, dry, and iron all vintage fabrics before you add them to your piece, so any changes that will happen to the fabric happen before you have spent a lot of time sewing.

For new fabric choices, you need look no further than your local sewing supply store. Once again, you want to find something that you think will blend with your project. In this case you can check the information on the bolt ends of the new fabric you are looking at and make sure the fiber content is the same as the vintage piece you are working on. Please, no polyester blends! Stick to the big five here. Try to keep like fabric together—cotton with cotton, linen with linen, and so forth. When you get your new fabric home, wash it at least twice to remove all of the sizing and throw it in the dryer so it can shrink if it wants to. Iron it smooth and you are ready to go.

Now it is time to choose thread. One of the easiest mistakes to make is to purchase thread that is too strong for the project you are working on. In this case stronger is not necessarily better. If you use a modern cotton-wrapped polyester thread on a vintage lightweight cotton, the thread is going to cause

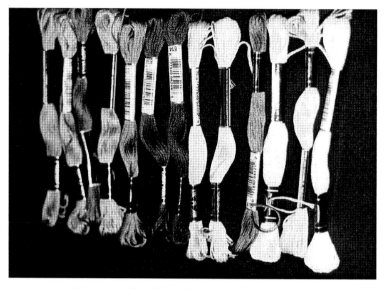

Cotton embroidery floss used in stabilizing

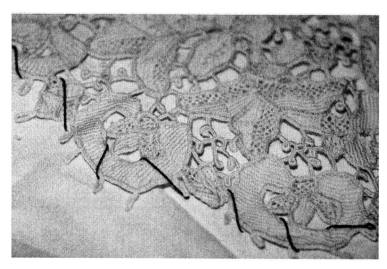

Stabilized fabric using cotton floss

the fabric to tear. Picture trying to sew through paper with dental floss; if you pull the stitches tight to fasten them, the thread will shred the paper. The rule of thumb is that you will always want the thread to rip in a case of stress before the old fabric does. You can always replace the stitching, but you do not want to lose any original fabric.

I often work with a single strand of cotton embroidery floss. It has some strength but generally will not tear a vintage fabric, it has no synthetic in it, and it comes in a wide range of colors. While this is generally no longer a problem, it is good to spot test red shades for color fastness. Wet a bit and rub it on a white terry towel. If you can see the color on the towel, the thread is not colorfast. Washing it before use will more than likely solve the problem.

Always use the smallest needle size that you can stand, to avoid poking big holes into a piece, and never use old, grungy straight pins. Buy some new ones if you have to, silk pins if you are working on a very fine or fragile item. Poking a large dirty straight pin into an otherwise clean piece will leave you with pin-dot dirt stains and can leave holes a little bigger than are easy to hide. The right size pin or needle does not break the thread when it goes through; rather, it pushes the threads out of the way.

Another way to stabilize a smaller item rather than patching it (on certain laces the cure can look worse than the disease) is to mount the whole item on muslin before washing it. Again, first wash the muslin a few times to get rid of all sizings and chemicals. Baste the small item onto the prepared muslin, using a single strand of cotton embroidery floss in a color you will be able to see later to remove. Use the largest stitches you can that will hold the piece still; you do not want to spend hours picking out basting later. Clean the whole thing as one, and when the item is finished, remove the basting threads and enjoy. You can always store the muslin for later use.

Now we are off to clean!

Chapter 4
Cleaning Without Washing

One of the aims of conservation is to make sure that anything that happens to an antique item is reversible, which is why there is so much resistance from conservators to washing or "wet cleaning" an item. If dye runs or a piece of fabric tears during the cleaning process, that is not reversible. You are pretty much stuck with whatever happens during washing. This is why I always say do as little as possible to any textile you own.

For this reason, and for ease, a lot of people send their vintage pieces to the local dry cleaner. This is not a good idea, for a variety of reasons.

The term "dry cleaning" is a misnomer. Liquid is used in the form of some harsh chemicals. Dry cleaning does little to remove odors and mildew, and residual chemicals left in the textile can actually hasten its decline. Unless a piece is spot treated before cleaning, and sometimes even then, the cleaning process can set stains, making them harder to get out than when you started. Often when I am in a household purchasing estate tablecloths I am told by the owner that there can't be any stains because the piece went out to the cleaner after its last use. These folks are often unpleasantly surprised by the condition of some of these items, first because the cleaner didn't get the stains out, secondly because the owner never opened out the piece when it came back from the cleaner and never really noticed, and finally because the cloths were left hanging in plastic for a long time—a very bad idea that we will address later in the chapter on storage. Finally, dry cleaning can be very expensive. While I would not recommend just throwing a 1930s rayon bedspread with silk and chenille trim into the washing machine, I would be careful about what I did and would not send it to a dry cleaner.

What are good prospects for dry cleaning? Drapes, for one thing. The cleaner can stretch them properly back into shape and can handle the fact that the linings and decorator fabrics may be different fibers or weights. Heavy bedspreads with bulky trim or bedspreads made of early rayon are also good choices for the cleaners; washing can ruin these pieces. Needlepoint pieces cannot be washed, and if they are stretched into terrible shapes the dry cleaner can block them back into original style. Some silk items may also benefit from careful dry cleaning, but the truth is, anything you can deal with without using the dry cleaners, you are probably better off taking care of yourself. Never send a quilt to the dry cleaners. The batting can soak up the chemicals for a very long time.

If you need to choose a dry cleaner, how do you go about it? First ask the local museum or historical society, to see if they have a recommendation. If that doesn't work, you will need to do a little detective work. Look for a dry cleaner that advertises French dry cleaning, because the French dry cleaning process is a little less invasive. Ask the manager or owner of the dry cleaning establishment if they have handled any antique or vintage pieces before. If the manager freaks out on being told that the piece is vintage, this is probably not the place to go. Even the best dry cleaners can't guarantee that there will be no damage to a vintage piece, but a competent one will not panic when you ask the question. Make sure the work is done on the premises, not shipped by truck to goodness knows where. At the very least, ask if your piece can be cleaned immediately after the fluid is changed in the vats. You do not want dirt deposits from other textiles added to your existing problems.

Sometimes having a good vacuum cleaner is better than knowing a good dry cleaner! On some items, including tapestries, needlepoints, items with three-dimensional surface embellishment, embroideries, fragile quilts, and so forth, neither dry cleaning nor wet cleaning is required.

Simply airing out an item can do it a world of good. Shake a sturdy piece out a bit to root out any little insect life that can be hiding in the folds. Gently smooth out a more fragile piece with your hand to see if anything is there that shouldn't be. A good airing can significantly lessen or even remove many musty odors.

Although direct sunlight should be avoided for display and storage because of its drying properties, it has its uses in cleaning. Mildew is caused when wetness creeps into a stored piece and leaves black and dark brown stains. Direct sunlight is the best way to counteract this problem. Sunlight will not remove the stain, but it can lighten it and will definitely keep it from spreading. Place a piece flat on a large sheet if you can, although in my neighborhood this is not possible because of the many cats and squirrels roaming about. I do not want any neighborhood animals using a vintage quilt as a litter box. Beware, if you live in an area with many overhead birds (pigeons, sea gulls, etc.) for the same reason!

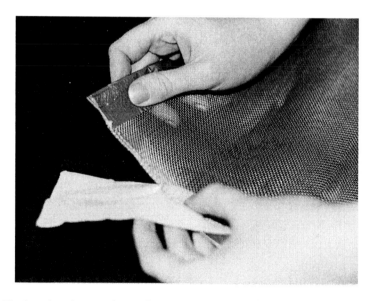

Taping the sharp edges of a screen to avoid damaging your textile

Hanging is all right if the piece can support its own weight without tearing, or you can mount smaller fragile pieces on a support of muslin. Do not leave any piece in direct sunlight for more than an afternoon, and make sure to expose both sides equally. Do not use this treatment for anything showing even the slightest signs of dry rot; sunlight will exacerbate this condition.

For items that are dusty but not otherwise in bad condition, air them first, then use your vacuum to remove the accumulated dirt. Go to the local hardware store and ask them for some window screen material. I use a piece about two feet square. I didn't even have to buy it; it was left over from a custom window screen replacement, and the proprietors were happy to find some use for it! Get some duct tape, gaffers tape, or heavy wide masking tape and tape over all four sides of your screen. This taping will keep the sharp edges of the screen from snagging your textile. Use two layers of tape if you need to. When you run your fingers around the edges, you should not feel the metal edges at all. Place the screen over the item you are working on and vacuum through the screen. This procedure enables the vacuum to lift the dust but keeps the threads or surface decorations from being sucked into the vacuum cleaner. On a thick piece, vacuum from the front and then again from the back. A small vacuum cleaner works well here. If you have only a large or very powerful vacuum, remove any attachments from the hose, get a piece of nylon stocking, and cover the hose end with it. Now vacuum through the screen using the covered hose.

Hopefully, airing and vacuuming will get your textile to where you want it without any further procedures. If so, skip to the chapter on storage. If not, continue on with me to washing.

Chapter 5
Washing

If you have expressed any interest in cleaning linens to any woman of a certain age, you have been deluged with tips. Boil linen with or without dish-washing soap, spot clean with lemon juice and salt and hang in the sun, pour boiling water through and then cover with salt—the list seems endless. Remember, though, that while this might have been sage advice when these items were new, you are now dealing with a 50-year-old or older tablecloth that cannot stand the abuse that a new fabric can. While lemon juice and salt, for example, may very well work on that rust stain, it may also leave you with a hole where the stain used to be. At the risk of repeating myself ad nauseum, it is always better to wind up with the remnants of a stain than to wind up with any kind of a hole. Don't court disaster with a harsh cleaning method.

What should you use? There are many effective cleaning products out there, but I will only address the most common. Keep an unbelievably soiled piece on hand on which to test new products. If you are told about a new home remedy or a new miracle product, try it first on a piece that you already consider a lost cause. If the new remedy doesn't work or creates a hole, nothing is lost.

Now let's review a few cleaning products and then examine some techniques for washing.

For vintage items with no obvious staining, as well as for quilts, the best product to use is Orvus Quilt soap. This soap is available at many craft supply stores listed in the resource section of this book. It is biodegradable, phosphate-free, and has no harsh cleaning agents. It will generally clear out in one rinse, which is also good. The more rinsing you have to do, the more agitation the piece goes through, and the more agitation the piece goes through, the more likely it is to rip. More details on quilt cleaning can be found in the chapter on quilts. For linens, use a tablespoon or two in a plastic container as a soak, then rinse once. While this product carries a warning to test on silk or rayon, I personally have had no problems washing these fibers in this product.

Sodium perborate is a cleaning agent found in several household soaps available at grocery stores. It is a white powder that can be purchased from archival supply stores and at some pharmacy counters. It is the product used by most museums and dealers when wet cleaning an item. Unlike soaps with sodium perborate available in grocery stores, pure sodium perborate has no perfumes, dyes, or sudsing agents, making it effective and easy to rinse. It works well on stains and yellowing but will have an overall lightening effect long term, so if you want to keep your item ecru in color instead of white, you have to keep an eye on this. Because it is slow acting (a good thing), you can soak items for up to a week or so, monitoring their progress so you can take them out of the soak when you are happy with the results. Dissolve two or three ounces—I use an old coffee scoop to measure—in hot water to activate it, then put the solution and the items into a plastic tub of warm water to soak. If the item is severely stained or yellowed, change the water when it becomes yellow or orange. It looks almost like a food coloring was put in. When you are happy with your results, rinse once and you are finished. Again, this product needs to be tested for silk or rayon, but I have not had any problems with this product and these fibers.

If you don't want to go through the trouble of purchasing pure sodium perborate, you can try soaking your items in one of the grocery store preparations. Ultra Biz is the most common. However, you may wind up rinsing two to three times after it is clean to remove all traces of suds and perfume. On a piece that can't handle too much agitation, wait until you can get your hands on some pure sodium perborate. You never want to store an item that has perfume, soap residue, or starch on it.

A product that I have had tremendous success with in removing food stains is called Oxi-Clean. Currently it is marketed primarily at home and farm shows, on television, and through direct-mail catalogs. I have soaked pieces in it and used it as a spot cleaner, and have had excellent results. In fact, I demonstrate it when I am giving lectures. It is only useful on cotton and linen, because it will eat up rayon and silk. I had a tablecloth with a mix of cotton and rayon fibers that I treated—I didn't know any better at the time—and it wound up looking like a weird lace! The cotton fibers stayed; the rayon fibers disappeared. This product only works in hot water and is only active for about six hours. It is very important to rinse this product out of the material when you are finished, and in fact on sturdier pieces I wash them with Orvus after spot cleaning to make sure all the Oxi-Clean is removed. I find it especially useful on kitchen tablecloths and towels from the 1940s and 1950s. It is great on food stains but does not fade the colors of the print.

Another anecdotal recipe is to boil linens in Cascade powdered dish detergent. While boiling in itself can be a great, if extremely time consuming, way to remove stains, Cascade and many other powdered dish detergents have chlorine bleach in them, which is very harsh.

Is chlorine beach ever useful in the treatment of vintage linens? A guarded yes is the answer. Chlorine is very harsh and will absolutely shorten the life span of any textile. Extended use harms the fibers, making the piece more prone to holes and thin spots. The more chlorine you use, or the longer you soak, the more likely you are to cause damage. However, if a white piece is so filthy that nothing else will work, is very sturdy without holes or dry rot, or you don't have a great emotional attachment to it but would like to see it come clean, then I would use a brief soak of chlorine bleach. It is a last-ditch effort and should be avoided whenever possible. My only personal exception to this rule is white, very sturdy bed linens with yellow lines from poor closet storage. A brief soak of fifteen minutes or so with one-quarter to one-half cup of chlorine per large washer load can remove these yellow stains quickly. Make sure to wash the items with a mild soap after exposure to chlorine, and make sure to run an empty load through your washer before you throw in your personal dark items.

These may not be the only products in the world that work, but these are the ones I use on a regular basis. If you want to try something new or not mentioned here, first read the ingredients. If chlorine is listed in the mix, you need to beware; less so with sodium perborate. Second, try the cleaning agent on a rag or something similar that is already damaged. If the cleaning agent is too harsh, you will not have ruined a piece that is important to you.

Now to the actual wash.

Need I say again the less done the better? I thought not!

Select the cleaning product you think will give you the results you want.

Choose a container to wash in, whether that be your washing machine, bathtub, or a small container. Your first choice should be to wash by hand in a plastic container, but obviously that is not going to work on a very large piece. Never wash in a metal container or washtub, because the metal in the tub can react with the cleaning product and leave you with worse stains than you came in with. Your washing machine tub is an exception to this rule. While it is metal, it is enameled or has some other water-resistant finish, so it is not like washing in raw metal. The bathtub is a great choice for washing out very large pieces like quilts, but you may have to schedule the family's washing-up times around your soaking, unless you have more than one bathroom. The washing machine is useful for large, sturdy pieces—sheets for example, or 1950s tablecloths. Again, though, if you are planning to soak for a while you need to schedule family wash times around that soaking. I was helping a neighbor wash out some nineteenth-century linen cloths that had been in her husband's family for generations but were orange with age and poor storage. Since she didn't want to tie up her bathtub or washing machine with the long soak that was necessary to clean these items safely, she bought a new huge plastic trash can, and we soaked them in sodium perborate outside in the yard. For the record, they came out beautifully.

Water temperature is dictated to some extent by the cleaning product you are using. While some experts think that putting fabrics into hot water will "shock" the fibers, this is something I have never experienced. I use warm water as much as possible, but some cleaners work better in hot, so that's the way to go.

Items in a cleaning solution can soak for anywhere from fifteen minutes to a week, so have an idea of how long you think something might need to soak and plan accordingly. Check on items in a long-term soak like sodium perborate at least once a day. If you are satisfied with the results, you are finished. Do not soak in a bleach for very long, and soaking in Oxi-Clean past six hours is a wasted effort.

Rinse all of the cleaning product out of the piece. The fewer rinses the better, but still be sure that all of the soap residue is gone. Squeeze clean water through the piece until it comes through clear.

Wax drips are very common on table linens and don't always disappear when laundered. The best trick is to lay a terry towel over your ironing board, then the item with the wax drip (wax side up), and then a layer of clean brown paper bag. Place your iron on a high setting and iron over the spot through the brown paper. The paper will get a greasy look to it, like it had potato chips in it for a long time. When you see that spot, move the paper so a clean spot is over the wax drip and iron again. Keep repeating until the paper stays clean. The wax gets into the brown paper and stays off the linen. If it was a colored candle instead of a white or beeswax one, you may have a little residual ink. Spot treat with an ink remover such as Amodex or Carbona for Ink.

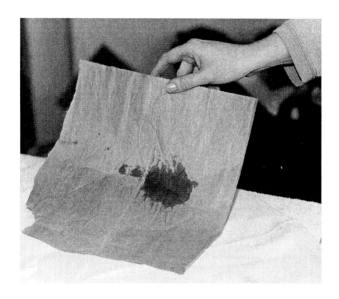

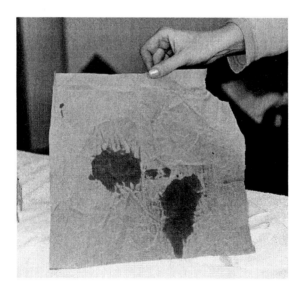

Removing wax drips on table linens. Repeat the procedure until the paper stays clean.

Chapter 6
Drying

So the wash is over, you have rinsed out all the soap residue, and you are now ready to dry the piece. The most important part of drying a vintage textile is to get as much water as possible out of the piece before you set it out to dry. Water is very heavy. No matter how you lay a piece out to dry, gravity will cause all the water to collect at the end closest to the ground. The weight of the water can cause stitching to pull out and break, especially in embroidered items and quilts.

The first thing you want to do is gently squeeze as much water as possible from your item. Notice I said "squeeze," which is not to be confused with "wring." Wringing implies a twisting action to get the water out, which can pull the item out of shape and break threads or decorative stitching. With squeezing, there is no twisting motion. You don't want to get too carried away here; just gently apply pressure from top to bottom to get the most water out of the piece.

Now that merely lifting it will not cause any damage, you can lift the item out of the container and use this next trick

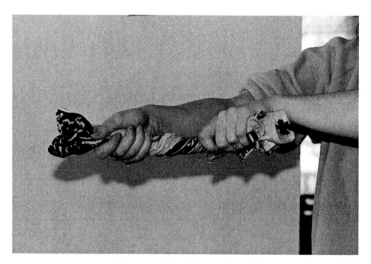

Wringing! A definite No-No!

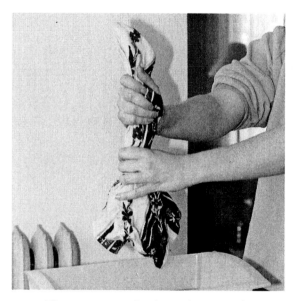

The correct method: gently squeezing

Use a large clean white towel and roll fabric up like a jelly roll

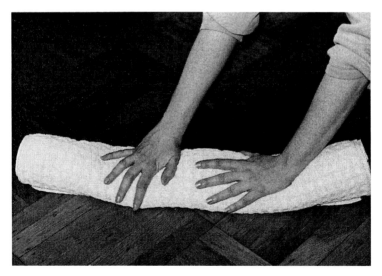

Press down firmly so that water will "wick" from the fabric to towel

to get a lot more water out. Take a large, clean bath towel (white is best, so there won't be any possibility of color transfer) and place it on the floor. Place the damp item in the center of the towel and roll it all up together like a jelly roll. Now press down hard or stand on it if you have something sturdy to hold onto so you don't fall down! The pressure causes the water to wick from the vintage item into the towel. When you unroll the towel, the item inside will be much dryer, making it easier to lay out to dry. You can then just throw the towel into the dryer.

Some larger, sturdy items can be placed in the washing machine and spun out using only the spin cycle. Be careful not to place too much tension on the item when placing it around the tub. You want to leave some slack, almost like putting it in a zigzag shape, so that during the spin cycle there is not too much pressure on the fibers.

Now that it is damp rather than wet, you can decide where to dry your item completely. Inside is better for smaller or more delicate items, but make sure air is circulating in the room where things are drying. A bathroom may be too humid, preventing things from drying completely, thereby allowing for possible mold growth. A basement may be too musty, allowing items to pick up a musty smell before they are completely dry. A basement or any other closed room will work if you have a dehumidifier going, because that will help items to dry quickly. Outside is terrific if you have a sunny day and a good place to put the item. Items dried in the sun must be pretty sturdy to start with; anything with early signs of dry rot will be better off if dried inside. Sun will make things dry quickly, but as soon as the piece is dry remove it to prevent fading or dry rot.

It is best to lay an item flat for drying because the whole item is equally supported, leaving no low-lying areas for water to collect. If it will fit on a plastic mesh sweater drying rack available from convenience stores and catalogs, so much the better. If the item is large, you may still be able to dry it flat. Lay it on a large clean sheet and put it out in your backyard. This method will not work in my neighborhood because there are too many wandering cats and squirrels, and I worry about them walking on or worse, defecating on my items. I once taught a class at the New Jersey shore where someone pointed out that overhead creatures may make messes on clean wash too! If bird doo is your main concern, you can lay an item on one sheet and cover it with another. For four-legged creatures or a lack of backyard space, hanging may be the way to go.

The case against hanging is gravity. Since a hung item is only supported in the center, the water weight will concentrate in the area nearest the ground, possibly causing damage. However, if you have no space or backyard to lay things flat, hanging is a must. In that case the jelly roll technique is most important, so you are hanging a damp item and not a wet one. Change the item's direction if you can. If the clothesline is running top to bottom, for example, change the orientation of the item after about an hour, so the clothesline is now running side to side. For a piece that will take a long time to dry, change it again later so the line is now on the diagonal. As soon as your item is dry, fold it neatly and bring it in.

Chapter 7
Ironing

The first thing you need to know about ironing is that it's not always necessary. If you are putting your clean vintage item into storage, you need not iron it at all. Proceed directly to the next chapter.

In general, ironing is a pretty low-risk procedure but, as always, don't do anything to a textile that you don't have to do. Ironing applies heat to the fabric, and heat can be drying. Save ironing the piece for when it's going to be used or displayed.

Make sure your ironing board has some padding and a clean cover. Make sure the face of your iron is clean as well; after all your hard work cleaning the piece you do not want to create new stains. Iron cleaning products are available at most sewing stores. Follow the label instructions. It is very important to make sure all of the iron cleaner is off the iron before you start to iron any fabric. Iron cleaner is very oily. If you are not sure that the iron is clean, iron over a clean brown paper bag. Any remaining cleaner will transfer onto the bag,

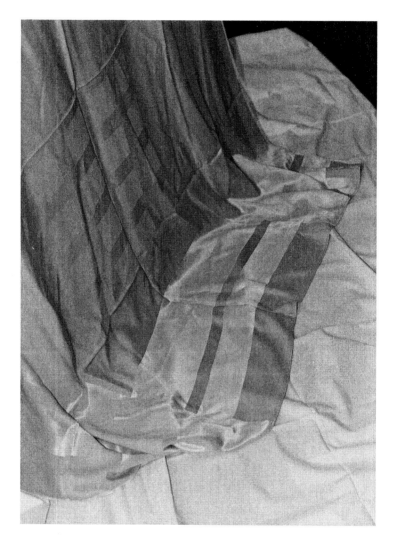

Ironing with a drop cloth. Spread an old clean white sheet under the ironing board to avoid any possibility of dust or dirt.

showing you a grease spot. Keep ironing the bag until no new spots appear.

Next, you want to make sure the floor under your board is protected. If a large piece touches the floor while pressing or you drop a small piece, you don't want to attract new dirt. This caution is not an insult to the state of your floors, just a fact of life: You don't want clean linen to touch where shoes have been. An old clean sheet works well here; just spread it under the board. Be careful not to track dirt onto your drop cloth while you are working. If you do get floor or shoe dirt on a piece that you are ironing, try removing it immediately by going over the spot with either a sticky lint roller or some strong tape wrapped around your hand. The surface dirt will stick to the tape before it has a chance to set into the fabric.

For ironing an item with embroidery that has depth to it—raised work or pad stitching especially—you will want to have a clean, thick terry towel available. Place the towel over the board, then the item to be ironed, with the right side of the work face down. Iron your item, being careful not to snag the point of the iron on the threads that often link small areas of embroidery on hand embroidery. By using the towel as padding, the embroidery will have somewhere to go and will not be pressed flat against the board. Press the plain areas of the piece again on the right side. This technique will make for a more attractive finish.

Cotton and linens can use a spritz of water while you are ironing, to smooth out the fibers and bring out the natural luster. A small spray bottle is best for this; you can find them at many stores. Don't soak the fabric, because that will make it easier to scorch. Just a light spritz over the piece and you are ready to go. For smaller items, spritz the entire piece before you iron, not just the area on the board. This will give the water a minute to soak into the fibers. I remember my mother spritzing my sister's school blouses and then keeping them rolled up in a plastic bag in the refrigerator until she had time to get to them. You can't keep things in there forever, though, or you are back to a mold problem. For larger items such as tablecloths and sheets, spritzing ahead isn't always possible. You don't want a wet item dragging on the floor.

The starch question plagues linen collectors and dealers alike. Although there is no question that a starched item displays beautifully, looking crisp and detailed, the fact is that in the long-term starch is not your friend. Over a period of time starch can cause yellowing, and if you starch an item before storing it you have made it very attractive to bugs, since starch is essentially bug food! Which is more important to you, looks or safety? That can change with time. If you are putting out a grand tablecloth for family dinner on a major holiday, you may very well want to starch. A good layer of spray starch can actually help prevent stains from soaking in, which is a good thing. However, if your piece is going into storage or is going to sit for a long time in an area where stains are unlikely to develop, don't use starch. The starch question often hits home when you are purchasing an item for your linen collection from a dealer or antique store. Unlike many of my colleagues, I do not starch my items before displaying them for sale. If you are going to take it home for your collection, or if it is going to sit as part of your stock for a long period of time (hopefully it is not!), do not take a chance on starch yellowing the item. Many dealers and stores do starch their items, and the items look lovely. If they are going out immediately for use in your home, that's terrific. If they are going into storage, however, I highly recommend rewashing the item to remove the starch before placing it in storage. This is not the most popular opinion I have ever put forward, but I am sticking with it.

Chapter 8
Storage

Now that you have become addicted to vintage linens, you probably have more items in your collection than you can display at one time. You also probably have a few pieces that you are saving or studying, rather than using in your home. And maybe you've even got a few that are too fragile to ever display but have sentimental or historical value. This chapter will address how to store these items to prevent further damage.

Any item that is going into storage should be clean and unstarched. Storing an item with a stain on it is only going to make the stain worse: The younger the stain, the easier it will be to remove. And as previously mentioned, starch on a stored piece can attract bugs and cause yellowing.

Think about how long this item may need to be stored. Something that you are going to display or use in six months will not need as much attention as something you will not be looking at for many years.

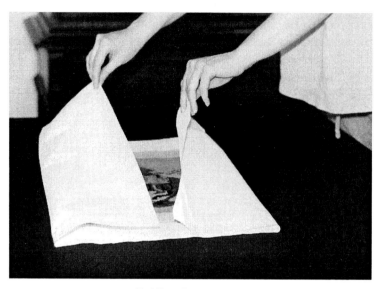

Folding for storage

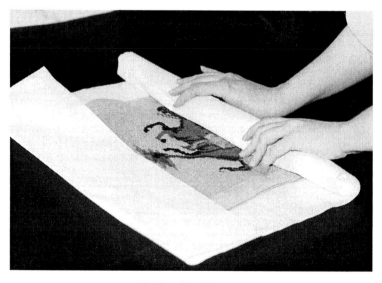

Rolling for storage

The first area to address is how to prepare an item for storage. There are three ways a textile can sit in storage. In order of preference these are flat, rolled, or folded.

One of the first places a piece can get damaged in storing is along the lines where it is creased or folded. The obvious way to eliminate this problem is not to fold it at all. That works great for smaller items such as samplers or lace collars, but you are limited by how much storage space you have.

For items that are too large to lay flat but are not huge, you can roll the piece up. Use the jelly roll technique we talked about in the drying chapter, with tissue paper taking the place of the terry towel. This works well for long, narrow pieces such as runners or lengths of fabric.

With a large item, such as a tablecloth or sheet, you will have to fold it somehow, unless you have a very large storage area. Fold as little as possible, perhaps folding the piece down to a size that you can then roll. In situations where a lot of folding is the only option, make sure to pad all the creases with tissue paper so they are not sharp creases. Try not to fold the piece the same way it has been folded for generations. Many large pieces I have found, particularly items like paisley shawls, have tears or stains in a grid pattern. This pattern is caused by the piece being folded in half and in half again, for example, every time it was stored. The area where the creases always were became weak and was more exposed to harmful environments. If you fold a piece in quarters the first time you pack it away, try folding it in thirds the next time you store it. If you always crease it top to bottom on the first fold, next time try side to side. Varying the folds in the item will extend its life.

Every textile you store should be wrapped before it goes into a storage container.

Sample archival storage boxes

Padding the crease of a large fabric with tissue paper

Without a doubt, the best storage containers and padding for storing vintage textiles are made of acid-free paper and cardboard. These products are used in museums and libraries to protect textiles and paper, among other things. I use them for my personal collection as well–things I want to keep for a long, long time. However, acid-free storage boxes can be expensive, so what can you do if you want to prevent problems with your fabrics but do not want to spend a fortune? I would invest in acid-free tissue paper. It is moderately priced and will prevent a world of problems. The next best choice is regular white tissue paper. Never use a colored tissue, even though our mothers often did. The color can transfer onto the piece you are trying to protect. On larger items where you would use a lot of tissue, you can wash and thoroughly rinse an old cotton white or muslin sheet and use that for an outer wrap or to pad. It is okay to thoroughly wrap an item and store it in a regular cardboard box, or on a shelf, or in a drawer, but with the following caveats.

1. NEVER STORE ANYTHING IN PLASTIC. The rule applies even if the container is sealed. Fifteen-gallon plastic containers on sale at the discount store have eaten more beginning linen collections than I care to think about! Have you ever gotten a loaf of bread home from the store on a hot day and found a ton of moisture inside the closed wrapper? The air in the bag went from the cool store to your hot car, causing condensation. Your bread (or your textile in a plastic container) is in a closed environment. Changes in the temperature of your home can cause a condensation buildup over time. Allowing moisture to develop can cause such problems as brown staining, mold, or mildew. If a plastic tub is positively your only option,

make sure to layer all sides, top and bottom, with tissue paper to absorb whatever moisture changes might occur. Check on it and change the paper layer with every change in the seasons.

2. NEVER STORE OR DISPLAY A TEXTILE IN DIRECT SUNLIGHT. Long-term exposure to sunlight will seep moisture out of the fibers of your piece, leading to dry rot, which is irreversible. Sunlight can also cause yellowing on the exposed areas. If you are hanging vintage curtains, make sure there is a layer between the curtain and the window. If you can, line the curtain; if not, use a sheer or glass curtain.

3. NEVER PLACE A TEXTILE IN DIRECT CONTACT WITH RAW WOOD. Wood contains acids, which seep into the textile and cause harsh yellowing. Even your new cedar chest, despite the label claiming it is oil free, will have a deleterious effect on any fabric. Every piece you place on a wood shelf or in a drawer should be wrapped in tissue, and there should be some extra sheets of tissue between the item and the wood as a barrier. Replace the barrier tissue every three to four months as it yellows. Don't forget the top of the pile in the drawer. I had a woman come to a lecture who had properly lined the sides and bottom of her wood drawer but had stuffed the drawer so full that the linen had come in direct contact with the bottom of the drawer above, yellowing the top item.

4. AVOID EXTREMES IN HUMIDITY AND TEMPERA-TURE. Don't store textile items in the bathroom closet where humidity and dampness might build up. Try to avoid baking your items in the attic, and avoid

the wild temperature fluctuations inherent in garage storage.

No matter how you store your linens and textiles, make sure to check on them periodically—at the very least once a year. Open the storage container, take everything out of wrappings, and check for damage and insects. Change the way the item is folded, if it's folded. Rewrap and put it back if all is well. Remember, if any problems occur it is best to know now and remedy them, not fifteen years from now when you want to use something or give it to your daughter or son.

The resource chapter at the end of this book will give you some places to shop for acid-free supplies. In the meantime, you can keep an eye out at house and garage sales for old plain cotton sheets to use.

Chapter 9
Quilts

This section will address some topics covered in previous chapters, however I wanted to put all the information specific to quilts in one chapter rather than putting it in dribs and drabs in other sections of the book.

Working with quilts is different from working with other textiles. Often the stitching or surface embellishments can make quilts difficult to clean, and their size makes storing quilts a challenge. Also, the quilts that we own are often the work of our grandmothers or other family members, and therefore have more sentimental value attached to them.

As always, and you have heard me say this before, the less done to a vintage quilt the better. With every process you put it through, you increase the possibility of damaging it. For a piece of extreme sentimental, historical, or financial value, please consider consulting a restoration professional. Do not send a vintage quilt to the dry cleaner, because the chemicals used in dry cleaning can build up in the quilt's batting and hasten its demise.

Once you have taken your quilt down from the attic or out of the cedar chest, you need to answer the question of restoration or conservation. Do you want to make it like it was or keep it like it is? In the case of a quilt, restoration might mean shopping for vintage fabrics to replace any missing or damaged patches, restitching any quilting that has come out, or rebinding with the fabric closest to the original color you can find. Conservation might mean covering the damaged pieces with a piece of silk tulle to preserve it, securing any trailing threads in the quilting, or using muslin to patch any areas where the batting shows through. In any case, the best advice is don't do anything that can't be reversed.

What is your quilt made of? Cottons? Wools? Silk? Does it have surface embellishments of lace or beads? Is the outside cotton feedsack material but the batting wool? All of these areas need to be considered before proceeding with a cleaning, because different fibers react differently.

What kind of damage has the quilt suffered? Are there stains, holes all the way through, missing patches, missing stitching? What needs to be dealt with and what can you live with? If you are going to use the quilt, it needs to be more stable than if you are going to store it. Examine your entire quilt and get an idea what problems need to be addressed, then plan how you will solve them.

A great way to look for holes is to hold the quilt up to a strong light and look through it. Your eye will jump to any holes because the light will shine right through, drawing your attention. And by the way, don't worry about any random dark spots that appear to be just in the batting but don't show up when you look directly at the fabric. These are probably cotton seeds!

For quilts that are musty but not stained, vacuuming and airing may be all you need to do. Go to the hardware store and ask for a piece of wire mesh window screen about two feet square. Cover all four edges with a layer or two of duct or gaffers tape, to prevent the raw metal from snagging any threads of your quilt. Lay the screen over a section of your quilt and vacuum the quilt through the screen. The screen prevents the fibers from being sucked into the vacuum cleaner or pulled out of place. A small hand-held vacuum works well here. If you don't have one, you can use the hose from your canister vacuum. Take the attachments off the hose and place a piece of old pantyhose over the end, securing it with a rubber band or more duct tape. The nylon will add some protection. Again, the idea is to avoid vacuuming the stitching or embellishments right off the piece. Vacuum both sides of the quilt, and really spend some time on it. You want to get as much dust out of the batting as possible.

Airing out a quilt can often improve its smell so much that nothing else needs to be done. If you have an outside area with enough space to lay it flat, that is the best choice. Spread a clean sheet down on the grass and lay the quilt on top of it. Leaving the quilt in the sunlight is fine for awhile, but be aware that direct sunlight in general is not great for any textile because it can fade colors and hasten dry rot. If you are concerned about roaming neighborhood animals pawing over your piece, you can drape the quilt over a line. But be careful that it is evenly supported, not hanging down too far one way or the other. You don't want the weight of the quilt to pull it out of shape or pop the stitching. If overhead birds are a problem, you can place another sheet on top of the quilt. Don't worry, the air will still circulate and help with odors.

If you need to wet clean, either by spot cleaning or immersion, be sure to stabilize any holes or missing patches first. If you are using a new piece of fabric to restore a quilt, wash the fabric to remove any sizing. If you are using a vintage piece of fabric to restore your quilt, you still need to wash it to remove dirt, to see if any color will run, and to be sure the repair piece is strong enough to do the job. Nothing is more frustrating than to do a gorgeous repair job that disintegrates when it hits the water, possibly as fast as the area you were trying to repair. Older fabrics are not color-fast like today's fabric are; reds and browns are particularly likely to run or bleed.

For a conservation project, you might want to patch holes with prewashed unbleached muslin. You can use the muslin to replace a missing patch or, if you don't want to go even that far, you can baste some muslin on to cover the hole during cleaning, then remove the muslin when the job is done. You don't want a flapping or missing patch to deteriorate further during cleaning or give any batting a chance to escape. Another quick fix for conserving a deteriorating patch is to stitch cotton or silk net or tulle over the area. This technique will help keep things from shifting without adding anything to the appearance of the quilt. This is great before storage, but I still prefer muslin, even if removed later, to prepare for a wet cleaning.

Be careful when stitching on a patch, whether it's to be temporary or permanent. Use a thread that is not too strong for the vintage fabric you are sewing. Contemporary cotton-wrapped polyester thread is very strong and can cut slices in your more fragile vintage fabrics. You always want the thread you use to be weaker than the fabric, so that if there is pressure to tear, the thread will break before the original quilt patch does. I use a single strand of cotton embroidery floss to repair quilts. It is strong enough to hold together but weak enough so it won't tear vintage fabrics. It's inexpensive and comes in a wide variety of colors.

Covering a hole with a prewashed unbleached muslin patch.

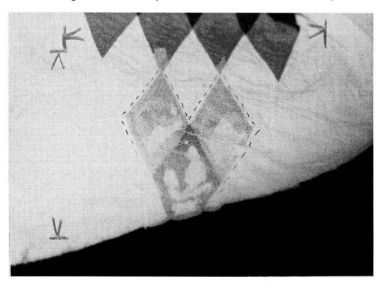

Using cotton tulle to stabilize a weak area

The only soap I recommend for washing quilts is Orvus. It is gentle, biodegradable, phosphate-free, and clean-rinsing. While not a stain remover per se, it is always amazing to me how much dirt it will lift in a short soak. It is not wise to use a very strong cleaner, because these can fade the colors over-all. Cold water is the temperature of choice for washing quilts, because it is less likely to run the colors or set in stubborn stains.

Before you wet clean a quilt that is too dirty or smelly to live with otherwise, spot-check colored areas for color-fastness. As I mentioned before, older fabrics can run or bleed when wet. Get a white, soft cloth or terry towel and wet a corner in a solution of tepid water and whatever cleaning product you intend to use. Gently rub the towel across an inconspicuous area of the fabric you are worried about. If color transfers from the fabric to the towel, *stop*, you are finished. Wet cleaning this quilt probably will cause more damage from transient dye than you had to begin with.

The big question in quilt cleaning is always where to do it. A bathtub is great to wash quilts if you can use it for a few hours to soak, wash, and rinse, but then you have the problem of removing excess water. A washing machine has its uses and is great for newer or sturdier quilts but is too rough on very old or fragile pieces. Sadly, there is no hard-and-fast rule for choosing where to wash a vintage quilt. I will give you the pros and cons of each, and you will have to decide for yourself, based on the individual piece you are handling.

If you are washing a quilt in a bathtub, be sure the tub is clean first! This may sound idiotically obvious, but because many bathroom cleaners today have bleach in them, it is imperative that there be no residue on the tub. You definitely do not want any form of any bleach coming into contact with your treasure, so if you have recently cleaned the bathtub you may have to rinse many times to be sure there is no cleaner residue.

The upside to using a bathtub is the lack of potentially harmful agitation. You can fill your tub with a solution of cold water and Orvus and gently place the quilt in it. Push it down into the water to let the soap go through it, *always being gentle.* You can let the quilt soak for 30-45 minutes, but do not let it sit too much longer than that. Gently roll the quilt to one side and drain the tub, squeezing (not wringing) the quilt to remove as much water as you can. Do not lift the quilt out of the tub when it is soaking wet, because the water is too heavy for the quilt to bear without damage. Refill the tub with cool water and spread the quilt out, again letting it soak for 30-45 minutes. Gently squeeze the water through it. If the water is dark brown with dirt, you may have to chance a second rinse. All the soap should come out on the first rinse, one of the reasons Orvus is so good for this kind of work. Roll the quilt to one side and drain the tub as before.

The downside of washing a quilt in the bathtub is the lack of ease in removing excess water. Especially in quilt cleaning because of the absorbant properties of the batting, water is the enemy due to its weight. Lifting a quilt that is waterlogged will put too much pressure on the stitching, often causing patches to separate or quilting stitches to break. Setting a very wet quilt out to dry is also a bad idea, because the batting will take forever to dry, leaving you with a good area for mold or mildew to develop. Squeeze—don't wring—as much water as you can out of the quilt while it's flat in the tub. If it still seems heavy, do not lift it out by itself because it probably can't bear its own weight. Place a long piece of prewashed unbleached muslin under the wet quilt and lift it all out together, letting the muslin support the weight of the quilt. If the quilt is relatively small or has a thin or nonexistant batting, you can lay it out on several clean, white terry cloth towels and roll it up like a jelly roll. Pushing hard onto the jelly roll will cause the water to transfer from the quilt to the towels. When you unroll the whole thing, the quilt should feel damp, not wet, and will be light enough to move on its own. On a larger quilt, or one that has a thick cotton batting, you might want to consider spinning it out in the washing machine to remove the excess water.

The advantage to using a machine to wash a quilt is twofold: You don't tie up your bathroom forever, and water removal is a heck of a lot neater. The disadvantage is that you *do* have to worry about agitation. It is great to use a machine that doesn't have an agitator, for example a front-loading machine. Some older machines that are top loading have agitators that can be removed. Removing the agitator is a fine idea, but beware what may be lurking underneath. Check for oil, ancient socks, or protruding screws that will eat your quilt for lunch. Use cold water and Orvus, soak the quilt 30-45 minutes if necessary, and then use the shortest wash cycle that you have. From here on out, you will have to stop the machine between cycles anyway, so if you don't have a short cycle you can physically stop the machine after a few minutes and move it on to drain the water.

Before the machine goes to spinning out, you *must* stop the machine and check the placement of the quilt in it. It is extremely important that the quilt be well balanced in the washtub. Besides the fact that you don't want this heavy, off-balance thing to walk your washing machine across the floor, if there is too much quilt on one side and not enough on the other, the centrifugal force used to remove the excess water will put too much tension on the lesser side, causing tears in the fabrics or on the seams. You need to carefully place the wet quilt around the washtub in an even fashion, leaving some slack along the way. On a rectangular quilt you want the length of it going around the tub, and you place it in almost a zigzag fashion. Then go ahead and start the spinning out cycle. After the rinse cycle, which should also be pretty short, you need to place the quilt carefully in the washtub again before the final spin.

The good news here is that the quilt will be relatively dry already and the possibility of it being damaged by water weight is very slight. You can go right from the machine to drying.

Please don't throw your quilt in the dryer. Different fabrics will dry differently, which can ruin the shape. The batting can ball up to nothing or get very lumpy, and any stains not removed by your gentle cleaning will be heat-set into eternity.

After as much water as possible has been removed from your quilt, you can dry it naturally, outdoors if you can, to speed things along. Drying a quilt is similar to airing, either laying the quilt flat (first choice) or hanging it on a line. If you must dry the quilt inside, you can hang it on the shower rod, as long as that is clean and the quilt is not too heavy. For a smaller quilt, you can lay it flat on a few mesh sweater-drying screens. Hopefully your neighbors all have one so you don't have to buy muliples!

Now that the quilt is clean, you have to decide whether to use it or store it. Vintage quilts look great on a guest bed or folded neatly and stacked on open shelves. Only use your most stable treasures, because even the gentlest sleeper is going to add to the quilt's wear, and an indoor pet may find it a wonderful place to play!

Some quilts make great wall hangings. Use prewashed, unbleached muslin to make a casing to run a rod through and attach both sides of the casing to the quilt. If you can, stitch the casing through the whole quilt, not just the backing. Supporting the entire weight of the quilt can cause the backing to tear. Put a casing on both top and bottom of a quilt, or all four sides of a square quilt, and change the direction it is hanging every six months to a year. This change of direction will ensure that any wear that occurs from being displayed is spread out and not concentrated in one area. Never hang a quilt in direct sunlight, because it will fade and dry out. If the rod you are hanging the quilt on is wood, make sure the wood is finished with some sort of laquer, or if it is raw wood, cover it with a layer of acid-free tissue paper before threading it through the casing. Change the paper every six months. Wood has acids in it that will cause fabric to yellow.

If you are going to put your quilt into storage, it is best to get some acid-free tissue paper and acid-free storage boxes. When you fold the quilt, crinkle up some tissue paper to pad all of the folds so none of the creases are sharp. Any textile wears more quickly along sharp creases than it does along a padded area. Don't always fold the quilt along the same lines. For example, if it's in quarters now, the next time you move it, fold it in thirds. This changes where the crease lines fall, and thus evens out the wear.

At this point, there is not much difference in storing quilts or storing other textiles, so return to the chapter on storage for a quick refresher course if necessary.

Chapter 10
Collection Management

Whew, I am exhausted from all that work we just did, aren't you?

Now that you have survived going through that massive pile of stuff your great aunt left you and have gotten a wonderful sense of instant gratification seeing how beautifully these items turn out when handled properly, you are a textile collector!

Take some time, if you can, to establish a written record of the items you own. Nothing fancy is necessary, a nice blank book or stack of index cards will do just fine. If you have gone to the trouble of rescuing these vintage items, you care about what future generations will do with them. The more information you can record about these pieces of history, the more fun you will have passing them on. For a small colllection, you need only describe the piece to identify it. For a larger collection you might need to start using a simple number system to label each piece. Record who in your family made it, how you took care of it, when you think it was made. Sometimes, even if a piece was not made by a family member,

#24

White Damask tablecloth   60" x 90"
Linen with urns and flowers pattern

Aunt Grace got it for a wedding present - 1936

Washed in Orvus and stored rolled   1/99
Checked and rerolled   9/99

#25

Printed tablecloth   52" square
Florida State Souvenir cloth

1950s

Brought at a garage sale 2/98 $5.00
Badly stained, spot cleaned with Oxi clean
    had to do it twice but now okay.

Stored folded in box #3   4/98
    checked and refolded   2/99
    checked and refolded   1/00

Sample index cards used for collection management. Although
these cards are typed, handwritten cards or entries in a book are
just as good.

the person who sells it to you will tell you its story. I try and remember all the details I can when I buy items for resale from estates where a family member is present. I am always amazed how my customers are hungry for details about those who created these beautiful items. Keeping a record of an item's care will help you in the long run, too, to remember what worked and what didn't and to remind you to refold something you haven't seen in a while.

I suspect that if you have become hooked on vintage linens you are suddenly seeing linens everywhere—at garage sales, friends' homes, antique shows, and auctions. While you might have walked by that pile of "dirty rags" at the local flea market a few weeks ago, now you will be pawing through it to see what can be saved! I am going to give you a few hints for adding to your collection with an eye to beauty and value.

Buy what you love and you will never go wrong. If your collection gives you pleasure and you are having fun assembling it, you are doing the "right" thing. There are no hard-and-fast rules about buying, but with a few pointers you will be shopping like a pro.

Garage and house sales are great places to start hunting for linens; almost everyone has some. When scoping out listings in the local newspapers, I try and choose sales in neighborhoods where the homes are older. I always hope old homes equal older linens! Another tip is if there is a sewing machine listed in the contents of the sale. I figure someone who sews is someone who is interested in fabrics, so maybe there will be some treasures there. Avoid items with holes. Damaged pieces are no bargain, no matter what the price, but as you get better at stain removal there will be many things to be had for a song because of stains that you know how to get out. Take chances here. If you are out a dollar or two, no big deal, but if you rescue something fabulous you are way ahead.

Antique shows and shops are the next places to look. There are dealers like me who specialize in linens and textiles, and many general dealers will have a tablecloth or two scattered in their display. You will probably pay more per item here, but the items should be in better shape, and you will have a better selection. If you are looking for an item for a specific piece of furniture, it helps to have the measurements. I can't tell you the number of times a customer has spread her hands to show me how wide the dresser is while I run for the tape measure! It is often okay to negotiate a better price than the one marked, but at least be polite about asking. Dealers always complain about those who are rude in asking for or demanding a better price, and I know from experience that even at a slow show I'd rather not sell a piece at all than sell it too cheaply to someone who isn't pleasant. Personally, I never object when someone asks, "Is this your best price?" (although it may be!) and I never discount to a person who starts a sentence with "I'll give you . . ." and proceeds to knock 40 percent off the tag price. A dealer will always have another show coming up and generally does not feel the need to discount heavily at the end of the day, even though that is a common misconception among the buying public.

Live auctions are a fun way to go, but beware. If you are an impulse buyer, this is not the place to be! The first auction I ever went to, I swore I wouldn't bid on anything, and I didn't. I sat and learned how things went and learned how to listen to the auctioneer. Each auctioneer has his or her own way of working, and once you get the hang of it, it's easy to understand, but sometimes the lingo at a local auction house can sound like a foreign language. With luck, if you are bidding your first time out, the lots you want are not first up, so you can see how the room works. Linens are hard to see at auctions and are often sold in several box lots. If you go to the preview early, perhaps a day or two before the auction starts, be sure to arrive at the auction well before it starts. Then make sure that the items you are interested in are still in the same lot number they were in when you saw them earlier at the preview. Items in box lots get moved around frequently, sometimes accidentally, sometimes on purpose. Nothing in auction life is worse than getting the box you wanted, at the price you wanted, only to discover when you get home that the cute cocktail napkins you really wanted are no longer there. Take notes at the preview so you can set in your mind before the bidding starts how high you want to go, and try to stick close to your limit, even if the blood-lust-must-beat-that-person-out feeling kicks in. Believe me, you will kick yourself later if you go way past what you wanted to spend, and that takes a lot of the fun out of going.

Internet auctions are exploding in size and scope, and there are literally thousands of vintage textiles available online. Let the buyer beware here, too. It's hard to do my "look into the light" trick if you can't hold the textile. I find a lot of misdescriptions online, too. I don't mean deliberately misleading the customer, although I am sure that happens, too, but people who aren't particularly knowledgable passing on wrong information. Look before you leap, ask what the return policy is before you bid, and for large purchases pay with a credit card if you can. As at a live auction, set your budget ahead of time and don't get caught up in last-minute over-bidding. Even in my auctions!

In addition to your favorite style of linen, what should you look for when adding to your collection? Remember, textiles are riskier than the stock market as investments, so buy what you love and only what you love. That said, keep in mind that some things are rarer than others and will always hold their value, regardless of the current decorating trends.

Buy the best piece you can afford at the time—the rarest, the best condition, the most beautiful. Quality will always show, and as your collection matures you can often sell pieces you no longer want and "trade up."

What should you avoid? Generally, items with holes are not collectible and do not hold their value, although there are a few exceptions to this rule. Crochet, no matter how beautifully executed, has almost no secondary market value and should not be purchased unless it fits in with your decor, although it's fun to keep and use the things family members may have made. Reproduction anything will not add value to your collection, nor will anything labeled "Made in China," even if it's from the 1940s and hand done. There is too much of it around to have any real value.

With many linens, size matters. Wider sheets are worth more than twins, 120-inch tablecloths are worth much more than 96-inch tablecloths, 30-inch square napkins are worth more than 24-inch square napkins. Because fewer items were made in the larger sizes than in the smaller sizes, there are fewer of them around, and their "rarity" value is much higher. In fabrics, it is very desirable to have a lot of yardage to reupholster period furniture. That's why 10 yards of fabric is worth more per yard than a 2-yard length of the same fabric.

One of the things you will see quite a bit of is damask—tablecloths, napkins, rounds. It comes in different fiber contents but a wide range of quality. There is all cotton, cotton/rayon blend (Post WWII), all rayon, and all linen. All linen is the first choice for collectors. Even in all-linen damasks, there were several grades or qualities. Some patterns, especially florals, were executed in different qualities of linen by the manufacturer so they could be sold in a variety of price ranges. The most common damask patterns are those with roses or chrysanthemums, therefore those are the least

A "figural" damask pattern. These are the most popular damasks to collect today.

valuable today. Art Deco and Nouveau geometric patterns are harder to find and fun to look for among the tons of florals. The most popular damasks to collect today, and for some time, are figurals. These are damasks that have a figure—a person or an animal—in the pattern. Mythological themes are popular, as well as cherubs or angels. Animals such as dogs, lions, and griffins (which is what I collect for fun) are also seen from time to time. These patterns are valuable both because of rarity and because (at least in Ireland) the figural patterns were only manufactured in the highest grades of fabric—a double whammy for the collector. Look for the biggest and most unusual pattern you can find in the glossiest of linen and forget the all-cotton roses.

Other styles of textiles come and go. What's popular as I write this may not be what people want by the time you read this book, so I won't go into trends. If there's a specific thing you love to collect, go for it. You'll just buy more when prices are lower than when they spike up!

Above all, enjoy your collection and pass the love of it on to a friend or relative. The more of us "rescuers" there are out there, the more lovely pieces will be able to be enjoyed in the future!

Resources

For questions about the information in this book, go to my
website at
www.marybethtemple.com

Books

Dating Fabrics. A Color Guide 1800–1960 (Paducah, KY:
American Quilter's Society, 1998) by Eileen Tesiain.
A terrific concept—this is a spiral bound book with many
pages of color photos of printed fabrics from different eras.
Especially valuable for assessing the age of quilts. You can
page through the book until you see a fabric that looks similar
to the ones you are trying to date. The spiral binding enables
you to hold the page right next to the piece you are trying to
identify.

*20th Century Linens and Laces. A Guide to Identification,
Care, and Prices of Household Linens* (Atglen, PA: Schiffer
Publishing, 1995) by Elizabeth Scofield and Peggy Zaiamea.

In my opiniion the best book of its class. Beautiful, clear pictures help you identify what you are looking at in your own collection, and the value guide is based on the authors' years of experience in the market. Nice historical notes without going into too much detail.

Conservation Supplies

Talas
568 Broadway
New York, NY 10012
Phone: (212) 219-0770
Fax: (212) 219-1735
Catalog available. Talas carries a wide selection of conservation supplies.

Metal Edge
6340 Bandini Blvd.
Commerce, CA 90040
Phone: (800) 862-2228
Fax: (888) 822-6937
Catalog available. In addition to a wide selection of conservation supplies, you can order a brochure on *Guidelines for Selecting a Conservator* which is published by the American Institute for Conservation of Historic and Artistic Works (AIC).

Glossary

Artificial Silk—The term given to rayon from the time it was first produced until 1924.

Basting—Stitching that is not meant to be permanent. The stitches are longer and looser than in a permanent row of sewing.

Batting—The thick layer in a quilt between the quilt top and the backing. Batting in a vintage piece is usually wool or cotton.

Bleeding—When a darker fabric's color runs (or diffuses) into an adjacent lighter colored fabric.

Conservation—Keeping things as they are: stabilizing an item so that no further damage can occur, but making no attempt to erase its flaws or damage.

Cotton—Fabric made from the boll of the cotton plant.

Cutter—A badly damaged piece of fabric (e.g. an embroidered or printed textile) that is perfect to cut up for craft projects or to restore other items.

Dry Cleaning—The process of cleaning an item with chemical solutions.

Dry Rot—A condition that results from a lack of humidity caused by poor storage. Even the gentlest handling causes the fabric to disintegrate. Dry rot is irreversible.

Linen—A fabric made from the center of the flax plant. Probably the oldest textile and the only fabric stronger wet than dry.

Muslin—A closely woven white or unbleached cotton cloth.

Pad Stitching—In embroidery, building up several layers of stitching over the same area so that the stitched area creates a three-dimensional effect. Often seen in dots and scallops.

Raised Work—In embroidery, stitches that stand up off the base fabric giving a three-dimensional effect; for example, French knots and coils of buttonhole stitches.

Rayon—Invented in 1894 as a possible low-cost replacement for silk; called artificial silk until 1924.

Restoration—Making things as they were. In repairing and cleaning an item, the attempt to make it look as close to its original condition as possible.

Shattering—When a fabric, especially silk, gets so dry that it disintegrates in vertical lines.

Silk—A fabric made from the cocoons of the silk worm.

Transient Dye——see Bleeding.

Warp—The threads running the length of a piece of fabric.

Weft—The threads running the width of a piece of fabric.

Wet Cleaning—The process of cleaning an item using water.

Wicking—The transfer of moisture from one area of fabric to another.

Wool—Fabric made from the fleece of a sheep.

Index